THE STORY OF
TITANIC
FOR CHILDREN

Joe Fullman

CARLTON KIDS

INTRODUCTION

Titanic was a wonder of its age: the biggest, most luxurious ship that had ever been built. It was famous even before it sailed. And when it rammed into a giant iceberg on its very first voyage, splitting in half and sinking to the ocean's depths, it became a global phenomenon.

It's difficult to explain why *Titanic* still fascinates people more than a hundred years after it sank. Other disasters have cost more lives, but it's *Titanic* that continues to hold the world spellbound. For one, the tragedy affected a lot of people at the time. The 1,517 people who died came from 33 different countries, making this a worldwide catastrophe. But the disaster also touched all classes. The ship was a floating palace made for rich holidaymakers, but it also carried hundreds of budget travellers looking to start new lives across the Atlantic.

The story of *Titanic* is, therefore, both a tale of how a giant ship was destroyed on its first voyage, as well as more than 2,000 stories of the people on board, involving daring rescues, brave sacrifices, escapes against the odds, near misses, tragic losses and more.

But, above all, it is probably the knowledge that the disaster could have been prevented that has kept it in the public imagination. For the sinking of *Titanic* wasn't an unavoidable accident. It was the result of a series of mistakes and blunders. One might even say the ship was sunk by the overconfidence of the people in charge. They knew they were heading into icy waters but chose to carry on. They had come to believe that *Titanic* was 'unsinkable' and could withstand anything nature could throw at it. But nature would have the last word in the shape of that fateful iceberg.

The Story that
Captured the World

On the night of 15 April 1912, the largest and most luxurious ship in the world at the time, RMS *Titanic*, crashed into an iceberg and sank to the bottom of the Atlantic. More than 1,500 people lost their lives in what became the most famous shipping disaster of all time.

The story of the 'unsinkable' ship has since been retold in thousands of books, television programmes and films. It's a tale that is full of drama, glamour, dreams of new beginnings, and acts of great heroism as well as cowardice.

MASS IMMIGRATION

The invention of the transatlantic steamship helped fuel mass **immigration** to North America. Throughout the 19th and early 20th centuries, millions of poor Europeans left their homes to start new lives in the United States. Until the 1920s, the USA had few restrictions on immigration, which meant that almost anyone could move there. The liners of the time, including *Titanic*, provided basic third-class accommodation for these immigrants.

The Statue of Liberty was many immigrants' first glimpse of the US.

STEAMSHIP TRAVEL

The origins of the *Titanic* disaster go back to the mid-19th century when the first large steamships capable of ferrying passengers across the Atlantic were developed. These grew in size over the decades and by the early 20th century they had become giant ocean **liners** that could carry thousands of passengers across the Atlantic in around a week.

White St...

LARGEST STEAMERS IN THE

LUXURY TRAVEL

In the early 20th century, crossing the Atlantic in a top-of-the-range liner had become one of the most luxurious ways to travel. Those rich enough to have first-class tickets enjoyed lavish facilities, beautifully furnished cabins and gourmet restaurants with an army of staff on hand to cater to their every need. The major liner operators of the time, Cunard and White Star Line, competed to attract customers to their ships.

A first-class stateroom (cabin)

THE LEGENDARY SHIP

Titanic was so enormous that people thought it must be 'unsinkable'. So when it sank on its **maiden voyage** it sent shockwaves around the world. Since then, the *Titanic* tragedy has been kept alive in countless retellings in film, television and other media. Interest in the disaster was further fuelled in 1985 when the wreck of the ship was discovered on the seabed nearly 4 km below the surface.

SHOWMAN'S GUIDE

Kenneth More in **A NIGHT TO REMEMBER**

A poster from the 1958 film *A Night to Remember*

THE ULTIMATE LINER

Titanic was designed to be the pinnacle of the transatlantic age. It was commissioned by White Star Line in 1908 to compete with two huge liners recently launched by another shipping company, Cunard. While the Cunard's main attraction was speed – in 1907, its ship, the *Mauretania*, set the record for the fastest transatlantic crossing at four days, 19 hours – *Titanic's* major selling point would be its sheer size and luxury. No expense was spared in its construction and fitting out, turning *Titanic* into the world's most famous liner, even before it had sailed.

A White Star Line poster boasts about the enormous size of its ships.

THE OWNER'S STORY

Founded in Liverpool in 1845, White Star Line grew to become one of the liner industry's most dominant companies. The construction of *Titanic* was the company's high point – followed swiftly by the low point of the disaster. Although White Star Line continued to operate transatlantic services for over a decade, demand for liner travel fell in the 1930s following a global depression and the subsequent rise of air travel. In 1934, White Star Line merged with its former rival, Cunard, to prevent it going bankrupt.

WHITE STAR LINE.

OLYMPIC. 45000 TONS. AND "TITANIC" 45000 TONS. THE LARGEST STEAMERS IN THE WORLD.

ALL STEAMERS BUILT IN IRELAND. QUEENSTOWN–NEW YORK ON THURSDAYS AND FRIDAYS. QUEENSTOWN–BOSTON ON WEDNESDAYS

For Freight and Passage apply to JOHN DENNEHY, Insurance Agent, CAHIRCIVEEN, Co. Kerry.

Poster advertising the regular sailings of *Titanic* and *Olympic*

Building
Titanic

Once White Star Line decided it needed a new mega ship, it was clear it would be built at the company's regular shipbuilders, Harland and Wolff in Belfast, Northern Ireland. Just over three years after construction began, *Titanic* was ready.

It had cost a whopping £1.5 million (around $260 million in today's money), but White Star Line could look forward to the profits they would make from ferrying all those rich passengers across the Atlantic – or so they thought.

BUILDING THE HULL

Construction of *Titanic* began at a Harland and Wolff **slipway** in March 1909. First the **keel**, the bottom part of the ship that acts as a sort of backbone, was put together from large chunks of steel. Next, curved steel beams were connected to the keel in a skeleton-like structure to form the ship's shape. Finally, giant sheets of steel were joined to the frame and to each other to create a watertight **hull**.

No. 193

"TITANIC
Launch.

To be retained for admittance to Stand.

Titanic being prepared to be launched in Belfast.

LAUNCH AND FITTING OUT

On 31 May 1911, the mighty ship was ready for the next stage of its construction. The empty vessel was launched down the slipway and towed to a different part of the shipyard known as the fitting-out wharf. Here, the engines and boilers that powered the giant craft were added, followed by the passenger accommodation and luxurious fixtures and fittings. In February 1912, the nearly completed ship was moved to a **dry dock**, where propellers and a final coat of paint were added.

A team of horses pulls the ship's giant 16-tonne anchor to the dockyard.

GIANT SCALE

Because everything about *Titanic* was done on such an enormous scale the shipyard had to undergo several adaptations. A vast new **gantry**, measuring 256 m long and 73 m wide, was created to hold the 16 cranes needed to build the ship. While the hull was being put together, a new dry dock was constructed, big enough to deal with the mega ship. It could hold 21 million gallons of water, which could be emptied in around 100 minutes by a system of giant pumps.

WORKERS

Around 15,000 workers were employed to construct *Titanic* and its sister ship, *Olympic*, which was built at the same time. That was around double the size of the normal workforce, and made the shipbuilder Belfast's biggest employer. It was, gruelling work, with the day starting at 6 a.m. and finishing at 5.30 p.m. The workers had only Saturday afternoons and Sundays off. It was also dangerous: eight people died during the ship's construction.

Titanic workers heading home in 1911.

THE SHIPBUILDERS' STORY

The shipbuilding firm behind *Titanic*, Harland and Wolff, was founded in 1861 by the British engineer James Harland and his German-born personal assistant, Gustav Wilhelm Wolff. It proved hugely successful, producing all of White Star Line's ships from 1871 onwards. Though it continued building ships after the *Titanic* disaster, business dried up in later decades. The firm made its last liner in the early 1960s, and its last ship of any sort in 2003.

The 'Unsinkable' ship

The tragedy of *Titanic* was particularly shocking because many people at the time thought the ship was so huge nothing in the world would be able to sink it.

It also had an ingenious safety system with a series of watertight compartments designed to keep it afloat should it hit anything.

A White Star Line brochure even stated that the ship was "designed to be unsinkable," while a passenger wrote to his relatives before boarding, "We are changing ships and coming home in a new unsinkable boat." It proved to be anything but.

THE GREAT SHIP

At 269.1m long and with a fully loaded weight of 67,000 tonnes, *Titanic* was the largest moving human-made object ever built up to that point. It had ten **decks** spread across a total height of 32 m, and could carry more than 3,500 passengers and **crew**. Though huge for its day, *Titanic* is comparatively small by modern standards. Some of today's biggest cruise ships are almost five times the size of *Titanic*.

A LA CARTE RESTAURANT

COMPASS PLATFORM

LIFEBOAT

PROPELLER

THIRD-CLASS ROOMS

SECOND-CLASS STATEROOMS

FRESHWATER TANK

ENGINES

COAL BUN

THE BULKHEADS

The features that were supposed to keep the ship safe from almost all dangers were located well away from the view of passengers. Fifteen bulkheads (metal walls) divided *Titanic's* lowest deck into 16 watertight compartments. The idea was that the bulkheads would prevent water from flowing into other compartments should one compartment start to leak. According to the designers, up to four compartments could become waterlogged and *Titanic* would still stay afloat. Tragically, the iceberg punctured five compartments.

Diagram showing how the bulkheads stretched across the bottom of the ship

FIRST-CLASS PROMENADE

THE BRIDGE

CARGO

FIRST-CLASS STATEROOMS

THE DESIGNER'S STORY

Thomas Andrews, the naval architect who designed *Titanic*, began his apprenticeship at Harland and Wolff aged 16. Just a decade later, he had risen to become the shipbuilder's head of design. He oversaw the building of *Titanic* and was aboard during its maiden voyage, to make note of any minor improvements that might be needed. When *Titanic* hit the iceberg, his in-depth knowledge of the ship meant that he was the first to realize it was going to sink. He helped many of the other passengers get into **lifeboats**, but was unable to reach safety himself and died in the disaster.

Loading
Titanic

***T**itanic's* vast size meant that it could carry a huge amount of goods, provisions and **cargo**. Much of this was needed just for the journey across the Atlantic.

Astronomical amounts of food and drink were required for the passengers and crew, including 36 tonnes of potatoes, 34 tonnes of fresh meat and 40,000 fresh eggs. The ship's giant **holds** were filled with passenger luggage, as well as tonnes of commercial cargo being transported to businesses in the United States. Last but not least, *Titanic* was also an official mail ship.

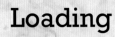

COMMERCIAL CARGO

Titanic carried more than 800 tonnes of baggage and freight. Commercial goods ranged from the industrial (cases of rubber, machinery and cloth, including cotton, lace and fur) and the practical (cases of soap, tissues and furniture) to the luxurious (8 cases of orchids, 63 cases of champagne, as well as numerous cases of wine, cheese and biscuits).

CARRYING THE MAIL

Titanic's full, official title was 'RMS *Titanic*'. The 'RMS' stood for 'Royal Mail Ship'. This meant that *Titanic* had been contracted by Britain's postal service, the Royal Mail, to deliver letters and parcels across the Atlantic. The mail was stored in the hold next to the first-class luggage. There was also a small mail room where Royal Mail clerks processed the letters and parcels during the journey.

A small boat delivers mail to *Titanic*.

LABELLING THE GOODS

The ship also had plenty of space for passenger luggage. Though some third-class passengers travelled with just a few belongings, many first-class passengers brought a lot of baggage. One first-class passenger, Charlotte Cordoza, had 14 large trunks, four suitcases and three crates loaded on to the ship. Luggage was stored in the hold and carefully marked with colour-coded labels to make it easy to find. The first-class luggage, in particular, needed to be simple to reach, as some passengers wanted items delivered to their cabins throughout the journey.

UNUSUAL ITEMS

This is a list of some of the more unusual items carried (and lost) on *Titanic*:

856 rolls of linoleum
76 cases of dragon's blood (a type of red dye)
2 barrels of mercury
4 cases of opium
3 cases of rabbit skins
A set of bagpipes
Renault 25 motor car (stored in parts)

A complete Renault 25

THE PETS' STORY

Twelve pet dogs were aboard *Titanic*. Most were kept in kennels down on the F deck. After it struck the iceberg, the kennels were unlocked, but none of these dogs were saved. Some smaller dogs were kept in the passengers' cabins. Three of these – two Pomeranians and a Pekinese – did survive when their owners insisted on taking them on to the lifeboats. The fact that they survived while so many people died created a lot of controversy after the tragedy.

ARTWORKS

The ship also transported several valuable artworks and artefacts. These included an autographed photo of the Italian revolutionary leader Garibaldi, a collection of 11th-century Persian poems called the Rubaiyat which was set with 1,500 precious stones, and a painting by the French artist Blondel, 'La Circassienne au Bain'. This picture later became the subject of the largest single insurance claim of the tragedy when the owner was awarded $100,000 to compensate for its loss.

TITANIC

THE FINEST STEAMER IN THE WORLD

One First Class Ticket to New York City, USA
Parlor Suite - £870

DEPARTING FROM SOUTHAMPTON
APRIL 10, 1912

SINGLE

Manning
Titanic

There were nearly 900 crewmembers on *Titanic* during its maiden voyage. The deck crew, including the captain, officers and storemen, were responsible for **navigating** and the day-to-day running of the ship.

Engineers, boilermen, firemen and electricians kept *Titanic's* thunderous engines running. Guests were taken care of by the victualling crew of stewards and galley staff, while entertainment was provided by two small bands.

ENGINEERING CREW

While the officers worked up on the bridge, the engineering crew had a much more dirty and noisy existence down in the bowels of the ship. Here a team of 25 engineers and 176 firemen and **stokers** worked to make sure the boilers were constantly fed coal, the engines kept roaring and the propellers kept turning. None of the engineers survived the tragedy.

THE OFFICERS AND CREW

The captain was the undisputed leader of the ship. He commanded a team of seven officers who assisted him in navigating and running the ship. Below them was a team of more than 60 deck crew including lookouts, carpenters, **quartermasters**, storekeepers, surgeons, lamp-trimmers and window cleaners. There were also 29 **able-bodied seamen** who had received special training to be able to operate and lower the lifeboats.

The captain and his officers pose for a picture aboard *Titanic* before departure.

STEWARDS AND STEWARDESSES

The 'victualling crew' was the official name of the 322 people who looked after the needs of the passengers. Acting as waiters, waitresses, maids and attendants, they performed a huge range of tasks from cleaning rooms, cooking and serving food, and maintaining toilets to washing linen, shining shoes and carrying luggage. There were just 18 female stewardesses. However, because women and children were loaded first into the lifeboats, 17 survived. Only 60 male stewards made it to safety.

Some of *Titanic*'s surviving stewards standing outside the official **inquiry** into the disaster.

FIRST CLASS
80
WHITE STAR LINE

AT YOUR SERVICE

In first class there was a gourmet restaurant operated independently of the ship by chef Luigi Gatti, who owned two high-class eateries in London. He employed his 55 Italian and French cooks, chefs and waiters directly. This meant they weren't officially members of the crew and were apparently prevented by stewards from getting on the lifeboats. Only three survived.

Isaac Maynard (right), one of the surviving *Titanic* cooks, arrives back in England.

CAPTAIN'S STORY

Titanic's captain, Edward Smith, was born in 1850 and began his seafaring career at the age of 13. By 1880 he had joined White Star Line and rose to be the company's star captain, commanding the maiden journeys of most of the company's new ships, including that of *Titanic*'s sister ship, *Olympic*. Normally known as calm and decisive, Smith delayed the decision to load and lower *Titanic*'s lifeboats for some time after it struck the iceberg. Perhaps he too couldn't believe that the giant craft was really sinking. He made no attempt to save his own life and went down with the ship.

The Journey Begins

By early April 1912, after three years of intense construction, *Titanic* was finally ready to enter service as a commercial ocean-going liner.

Following a short **sea trial** near Belfast, the ship set sail to pick up provisions and passengers for its first trip from Southampton in the UK to New York in the United States. Not everything went to plan, and the ship narrowly avoided crashing into another boat in Southampton. Indeed, after the tragedy, many people came forward claiming to have had **premonitions** of the disaster. But for the first few days all seemed to be well as the ship made stops in France and Ireland before heading out into the Atlantic Ocean.

SEA TRIALS

The first time *Titanic* moved under its own power (rather than being pulled by a tug) was during its sea trial of 2 April 1912. It lasted just a few hours. The ship's engines were run at full power, allowing it to reach a top speed of 21 **knots** (38 km/h). Its turning ability was tested and it performed an emergency stop, coming to a standstill after 3 minutes, 15 seconds, having travelled 777 m. Having performed well, the ship departed that day for Southampton.

Titanic looked impressive as it made its first sea journey.

New York

BOARDING

Having travelled overnight from Belfast, *Titanic* arrived in Southampton on 3 April 1912. Over the next week, thousands of tonnes of provisions and cargo were brought aboard and the crew got ready for the transatlantic journey. Boarding began on the morning of 10 April, giving many passengers their first awestruck glimpse of the giant ship. Finally, just after midday, the gangplank was drawn up, the engines were fired up and the ship headed out of the dock.

Friends and family wave goodbye to passengers boarding the ship.

UNDERWAY

As the first 922 passengers from Southampton excitedly got to know their new surroundings, the ship made its way across the English Channel to Cherbourg, France, where it picked up a further 274 passengers. It then turned back and made its penultimate stop in Queenstown, Ireland, on the morning of 11 April where the final passengers boarded, making a grand total of over 1,300. By early afternoon, the ship was ready to depart and steamed out into the Atlantic heading for New York.

MISSING THE BOAT

Not everyone who had tickets for *Titanic* made the trip. This included the chairman of Harland and Wolff, William Pirrie, who was ill, Milton S. Hershey, the founder of a US chocolate company, who cancelled for business reasons, and Guglielmo Marconi, the wireless pioneer, who had been offered a free ticket as thanks for supplying the ship's radio **telegraph** and operators. However, he had already booked a trip on Cunard's *Lusitania*, *Titanic's* rival liner.

Milton S. Hershey

Queenstown
(Cobh)

BELFAST

QUEENSTOWN
(COBH)

SOUTHAMPTON

Left: the intended route of *Titanic*.

CHERBOURG

PREMONITIONS OF DISASTER

Two books seemed to have foreseen the disaster with eerie accuracy more than a decade before it happened. *Futility or the Wreck of the Titan* by Morgan Robertson, written in 1898, tells the story of a ship hitting an iceberg and sinking while crossing the Atlantic. But the book *From the Old World to the New* by William T. Stead was even more uncanny. It tells the story of a ship sunk by an iceberg in the Atlantic. Survivors were rescued by a boat captained by an E.J. Smith, the same name as *Titanic's* captain. And, as a final spooky twist, Stead actually sailed, and lost his life, on *Titanic*.

Titanic prepares to leave Belfast on its maiden voyage, 10 April 1912.

FUTILITY
THE WRECK of THE TITAN

MORGAN ROBERTSON

Powering
Titanic

As well as being the top luxury liner, *Titanic* was also a monstrous machine. To power the craft, its shipbuilders, Harland and Wolff, had built some of the biggest engines and propellers yet. But contrary to rumours at the time, the ship was not designed to be supremely fast.

People thought that White Star Line wanted *Titanic* to break the record for a transatlantic crossing set by *Mauretania* a few years before. In fact, the ship's top speed was around 4 knots (7 km) slower than its rival's. Its main appeal was splendour, not speed.

THE BOILERS

Twenty-nine boilers containing 159 individual furnaces kept *Titanic's* engines running. Members of the crew called stokers had to work around the clock, constantly feeding the engines and getting through a staggering 660 tonnes of coal a day. In total, *Titanic* could carry 5,997 tonnes of coal. However, a strike by local coal miners just before its departure meant that on its maiden voyage it carried only 5,345 tonnes – still more than enough to get safely across the Atlantic.

THE ENGINES

Titanic was driven by three colossal propellers at the rear of the ship. The outer propellers were powered by two massive steam engines. Standing over 9 m tall, they were the largest engines of their type built at that time. The central propeller was powered by another monster, a 427-tonne turbine engine. Together, the engines and propellers could produce a top speed of 24 knots (44 km/h).

The enormous engine was supported by a massive A frame.

THE PROPELLERS

Made of cast bronze, the two outer propellers had three blades and measured 7 m across. They could spin in either direction, allowing the ship to turn left or right, or to go into reverse. The central propeller was smaller, just 5 m across, and had four blades. It could only go in one direction and was used mainly to boost the ship's speed when it was sailing in clear water. The propellers proved so hard and durable that the right-hand (or **starboard**) propeller was found almost perfectly preserved on the seabed more than 70 years after the disaster.

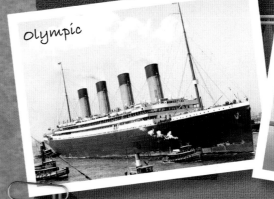

Olympic

Britannic

Workers inspect the giant propellers.

THE SISTERS' STORIES

Such has been the level of *Titanic's* fame – both before and after the disaster – that it's often forgotten that it was one of three almost identical ships commissioned by White Star Line at the same time. The first to be completed was *Olympic* in 1911. Despite a minor collision with another ship on its fifth voyage, it made many successful transatlantic trips before being retired and broken up in 1935. The final ship, *Britannic*, had a less happy story. Completed just as the First World War started, it was turned into a hospital ship by the British military. On 21 November 1916, *Britannic* struck a mine near Greece and sank, killing 30 people.

THE FUNNELS

On top of *Titanic* were four gigantic funnels. The first three took away smoke and fumes produced by the boilers. They were built very tall, rising 19 m above the top deck, so that the fumes would be released high up in the air to be carried away by the wind – any lower and passengers on the top deck risked being covered in soot. The rear funnel was actually a 'dummy' funnel, built to make the ship look more impressive, although it also provided ventilation for the engine room.

Smoke pours from the three 'real' funnels.

The Luxury Liner

***T**itanic* was a floating palace with first-class interiors that rivalled the grandest hotels. Its lavish facilities included restaurants, saloons, libraries, special walking areas called promenades and a heated swimming pool.

Everything was purpose-built for the ship and of the highest quality, from the crystal chandeliers and gold-plated light fittings to the bone-china crockery and Moorish-style tiles in the **Turkish bath**.

THE A LA CARTE RESTAURANT

There were other dining options for first-class passengers. Café Parisien on B Deck served the same menu as the dining room, but had a more relaxed feel and was popular with younger passengers. With its 18th-century style décor, thick carpets, large windows and flower-covered tables, the splendid A La Carte Restaurant, also on the B Deck, was given the nickname 'The Ritz' by passengers. It served up a high-class menu of caviar, lobster and other exclusive meals.

DINING FACILITIES

Titanic's first-class dining saloon was the place to be at mealtimes. Taking up the entire width of the boat, it could seat more than 500 diners and was ornately decorated with oak furniture, lamps and linoleum tiles designed to look like a Persian carpet. Evening meals were signalled by the ship's **bugler** who played a traditional song called 'The Roast Beef of Old England' to call diners to the saloon. Both men and women dressed in their finest clothes for the seven-course meals, after which there was usually dancing.

PLACES TO GATHER

When not sitting down to multi-course meals, first-class passengers had plenty of other spaces to relax and enjoy the high life. These included the top boat deck (so called because this was where the lifeboats were kept). There was also a smoking room (for men only) and a reception hall where drinks were served and a small orchestra played during tea (from 4–5 p.m.) and again after dinner (from 8–9 p.m.).

STATEROOMS

The staterooms, as the ornately decorated first-class private cabins were known, ranged in size from single rooms to giant suites with dressing rooms, private bathrooms and private **promenade decks**. They were spread over five decks in the middle of *Titanic* where the ship's rolling and swaying would be felt the least. In between the more luxurious rooms were some simpler cabins where the first-class passengers' servants and staff stayed, ready to perform their employers' wishes at a moment's notice.

THE FINANCIER'S STORY

When *Titanic* took to the seas in 1912, J.P. Morgan, the American banker and one of the wealthiest men in the world, was supposed to be on it. After all, he had been largely responsible for funding its construction. In 1902, he had founded the International Mercantile Marine Company (IMM), which took control of several existing shipping lines, including White Star Line. However, he cancelled at the last minute, and died the following year of natural causes. The IMM, however, never recovered from the *Titanic* disaster and went bankrupt in 1915.

RELAXATION

In order to keep its guests in the best condition for tackling all those meals, *Titanic* had a squash court and a gymnasium with a rowing machine and exercise bikes – facilities offered on few other boats. For some real relaxation, there was also a Moorish-style Turkish bath with a sauna and a 10 m pool. Filled with seawater, the pool was warmed to room temperature by the ship's boilers. After their exercise, passengers could get even their hair cut and styled at the first-class barbershop.

All Aboard

First Class

White Star Line spent a fortune turning *Titanic* into the finest and most luxurious liner of its time in order to attract some of the world's wealthiest passengers.

The first-class passenger list included several members of the British aristocracy, as well as leading politicians, businessmen and industrialists. Many brought along teams of servants. A basic first-class ticket cost £30 (about £1,110 in today's money) while a top-of-the-line suite was a whopping £870 (around £32,000 in today's money). There were 329 first-class passengers on *Titanic*.

MAKING AN ENTRANCE

Even the wealthiest passengers, used to living in the lap of luxury, would have been impressed by the ship's grand staircase. It was a strikingly opulent structure with oak panelling, intricately carved balustrades, a clock, paintings and gold-plated light fittings. Topped by a glass dome, it swept down from the promenade deck to the first-class dining saloon. At its foot stood a bronze cherub holding a lamp. The grand staircase has featured in almost every film made about *Titanic*.

The grand staircase was one of the ship's most famous features.

GOING DOWN

White Star Line didn't want its first-class guests to tire themselves out with all that walking up and down the grand staircase. So they installed three ornately decorated lifts just in front of the stairs. They were equipped with attendants to press the buttons, and comfortable sofas for guests to rest their feet during the brief journey down the five decks to their cabins.

THE ASTORS

American businessman John Jacob Astor IV, the owner of New York's Astoria hotel, the 'world's most luxurious hotel', was the richest person on board, and one of the richest people in the world at the time. Aged 47, he was returning to the US with his pregnant 18-year-old wife Madeleine. After the ship struck the iceberg, Astor helped his wife into a lifeboat, and then stayed on deck waiting for the time when men could start to board. That time never came and he went down with the ship. His body was recovered from the water on 22 April 1912.

THE DUFF GORDONS

British aristocrat Sir Cosmo Duff Gordon and his fashion designer wife Lucy, Lady Duff Gordon, boarded Titanic as two of its most celebrated passengers. After the tragedy, however, they became notorious figures. They escaped in Lifeboat 1, which carried just 12 passengers even though it had a capacity of 40. Sir Cosmo was called a coward for taking his place before all the women and children had been saved. Worse, he was accused of bribing the crew not to return to rescue people in the water. An inquiry officially cleared him, but his reputation never recovered.

THE COUNTESS AND THE CREWMAN

Britain had a strict class system in 1912. In normal circumstances, a member of the aristocracy would never spend time with someone of a lower class. But the evacuation of Titanic was not a normal circumstance. Lady Noël Martha, Countess of Rothes was put in Lifeboat 8. There she was given the job of steering by Able Seaman Thomas Jones, who was in charge of the boat. All 36 people in the boat made it to safety. Afterwards, the countess gave the seaman a silver watch as a thank you, and the pair wrote each other letters for the rest of their lives.

Second- and Third-class Facilities

Facilities in second class may not have been as good as those in first, but they were still much better than the first-class facilities of many other ships of the period.

Cabins were comfortable and spacious, the dining room served generous four-course meals and there was an oak-panelled library and a promenade deck to relax on. *Titanic* was also the first ship to install an electric lift in second class. Things were a little rougher in third class. Couples, families and single women stayed in small, cramped cabins, while single men shared communal **dormitories**. Public spaces were very basic.

A second-class room with bunk beds, sofa and desk

Travelling
Second Class

Travelling second class on *Titanic* was by no means harsh. The cabins were extremely comfortable with portholes providing natural light. They slept two to four people in beds or bunks and had items of furniture, such as sofas, wardrobes or writing desks. The dining room had mahogany swivel chairs, long tables and oak panelling. Many second-class passengers would have changed into formal evening wear for dinner, just like their counterparts in first class.

Third Class

There were just a few simple public rooms available to third-class passengers, including a smoking room and a general room (or lounge) with wooden benches. Simple meals were taken in shifts in the third-class dining saloon, which had room for only 434 diners. This in itself was quite a novelty. On most other liners, third-class passengers were expected to bring their own food. On *Titanic*, third-class passengers could even take a bath, although they'd have to wait their turn. There were only 2 bathtubs for more than 700 passengers.

A replica third-class room with four beds, a wash basin, and electric light

Taking the Air
Second Class

As in first class, second-class passengers had access to the top boat deck and their own special enclosed promenade deck just below it. These areas were equipped with benches and deck chairs and illuminated at night by electric lights. Passengers would come here to stroll and socialize in the sea air, drink tea and coffee, and perhaps even play deck games. There was plenty of space – in fact the *Titanic's* fatal lack of lifeboats meant that the boat deck was more spacious than it should have been.

Third Class

Third-class passengers had the worst outdoor facilities. They shared their area with various pieces of cargo and equipment and were provided with only hard wooden benches. It was located at the rear of the ship, so if the wind was blowing in the wrong direction, passengers would also have to deal with smoke billowing from the funnels. Still, it would have made a welcome change from the crowded conditions inside the boat.

The Phillips' Story

Second-class passengers Robert Phillips and his daughter Alice had decided to emigrate to the US after the death of Robert's wife in 1911. Robert's brother in Philadelphia had offered him a job in his factory, so Robert bought tickets for the transatlantic trip on a ship called the SS *Philadelphia*. Unfortunately, a coal miners' strike meant the *Philadelphia* couldn't sail, and the father and daughter were transferred to *Titanic* instead. When the ship struck the iceberg, Alice was evacuated in Lifeboat 12. Her father went down with the ship.

Travelling in
Second and Third Class

The 285 second-class passengers on *Titanic* were mainly holidaymakers and business people. They included teachers, priests, farmers and carpenters, as well as maids and chauffeurs for those travelling in first class.

Most had paid about £13 (around £100 in today's money) for their ticket. The majority of the 710 passengers in the cheapest third-class accommodation were not going on holiday. Most had a one-way ticket, costing £7 (around £65 today) and a simple plan: to start a new, better life in North America.

Titanic's musicians, who all perished in the sinking

Teacher Lawrence Beesley

THE SCHOOLTEACHER

Lawrence Beesley was a typical second-class passenger. A teacher by profession, he had bought his *Titanic* ticket in order to take a holiday in the US. As the boat began to sink, he escaped in Lifeboat 13, and went on to publish one of the first books about the disaster, *The Loss of the Titanic*, just nine weeks later. He also attended the filming of the 1958 movie about *Titanic*, *A Night to Remember* – and tried to join the cast during the sinking scene, but was removed by the director.

'The best first-hand account of a passenger's experiences'
THE GUARDIAN

THE LOSS OF THE TITANIC

'I Survived the TITANIC'

'Remarkable for its vividness & completeness'
THE DAILY EXPRESS

'The clearest account given by any survivor of the disaster'
THE DAILY MAIL

LAWRENCE BEESLEY

THE BAND PLAYED ON

Titanic's first-class passengers were entertained by two bands: a string quintet and a trio made up of a violinist, a cellist and a pianist. All eight musicians travelled in second class. On the night of the disaster, they came together as a single band in the first-class lounge. Here they played a selection of hymns and popular hits to try to calm the other passengers. According to witnesses, they carried on playing right to the end. All lost their lives.

An advertisement for *Titanic's* musicians

THE *TITANIC* ORPHANS

The French second-class passenger Michel Navratil boarded *Titanic* using a false name, Louis Hoffman. He had recently split up from his wife, Marcelle, who had been given custody of their two young boys, aged two and three. Greatly upset, Michel kidnapped the boys with the intention of running to the US to start a new life. Although Michel died, the children were saved in a lifeboat. However, because Michel had also given them false names, nobody knew who they really were. Thankfully, Marcelle saw a picture of the '*Titanic* orphans' and travelled to the US to claim them.

THE CHILD'S STORY

As many other passengers, the Hart family, made up of father Benjamin, mother Esther and 7-year-old daughter Eva, was due to sail to the US on SS *Philadelphia*, but a coal strike saw them transferred to *Titanic*. Esther felt that people were tempting fate by calling the ship 'unsinkable', so she stayed up at night to keep watch. When *Titanic* hit the iceberg, the family rushed out on deck. As Benjamin helped his wife and daughter into Lifeboat 14, he said to Eva, "Hold Mummy's hand and be a good girl." Those were the last words he ever spoke to her.

A NEW LIFE

Most third-class passengers were from the UK, Ireland and Scandinavia, although there were also people from as far afield as Eastern Europe, Russia and even Australia on board. What linked them was their poverty, with most moving to the US in the hope of changing their fortunes. Many large families were on board, including John and Annie Sage who had nine children. There were also several mothers and wives travelling alone or with their children on their way to meet up with husbands who had gone ahead to find work in the US.

Eva Hart with her parents and in her home in 1992

Crossing the
Atlantic

Between the afternoon of Thursday 11 April, when *Titanic* left Ireland, and the evening of Sunday 14 April, the ship made good progress across the Atlantic.

The weather was calm and passengers spent their time getting to know the ship and making use of the facilities, taking the sea air and writing letters home. As the ship approached the north-west Atlantic, however, temperatures began to drop. *Titanic* received a number of warnings that icy seas lay ahead. Still, no one believed the ship was in any real danger.

PASSING THE TIME

Titanic was due to take eight days to reach New York, so passengers had to find plenty of ways of passing the time. Of course, first-class passengers could enjoy the ship's swimming pool, gymnasium, squash court and Turkish bath. And both first- and second-class passengers could also play deck games, such as shovelboard and quoits, as well as board games. However, there were fewer options for those in third class, although many chose to fill their time by playing cards.

A pack of official White Star Line playing cards

KEEPING IN TOUCH

Passengers on *Titanic* weren't completely isolated from the outside world. Many wrote letters and postcards, some of which were delivered after the ship's stop at Queenstown, Ireland. Others made use of a new invention – the radio telegraph. There were two wireless operators aboard the ship who sent and received messages with a **Morse code** transmitter in a small office. Although the operators' main job was to communicate with other ships and coastguards about possible dangers, they also sent personal messages from passengers to shore.

Wireless operators, Jack Phillips and Harold Bride

EARLY WARNINGS

As *Titanic* made its way across the Atlantic, it received numerous warnings of icy conditions from other ships both by telegraph and signal lamp, including seven on the day of the 14th alone. The telegraph operators would have decoded each message, logged it and then passed it on to the officers on the bridge. One message, from a ship called the *Caronia*, warned of 'bergs, growlers and field ice' in *Titanic's* way. Yet the ship's officers seemed unconcerned and made no attempt to alter their course or speed.

FULL STEAM AHEAD

Perhaps the crew really did believe that the ship was unsinkable. Or maybe the early part of *Titanic's* journey had been so trouble-free that it gave the crew a false sense of security. Certainly the captain believed the ship was in no danger. Nor did Bruce Ismay, the chairman of White Star Line. He was on board and wanted the ship to arrive a day early in order to get good publicity. And so the ship sped on.

Bruce Ismay, chairman of White Star Line

POSTAL TELEGRAPH — COMMERCIAL CABLES

RECEIVED AT
POSTAL TELEGRAPH BUILDING
1315 PENNSYLVANIA AVENUE
WASHINGTON, D.C.
TELEPHONES MAIN 6600-6601

CLARENCE H. MACKAY, PRESIDENT

TELEGRAM

DELIVERY No
795

The Postal Telegraph-Cable Company (Incorporated) transmits and delivers this message subject to the terms and conditions printed on the back of this blank

DESIGN PATENT No. 40529

280 Ny.Rn. 22

S S Amerika via S S Titanic and Cape Race N.E. April,14,1912

Hydrographic Office,Washington DC

Amerika passed two large icebergs in 41 27 N 50 .8 W on the 14th of April

Knutp,10;51p

62496 filed with 2995

HYDRO. OFFICE
Rec'd APR 15 1912

Enclosures

Telegraph 3 1d. o New york
April 15, 1912.
P.C.

Telegram from the SS *Amerika* warning the *Titanic* of 'large icebergs' ahead

THE PERFUMER'S STORY

German-born Adolphe Saalfield was a perfume maker living in Manchester. He bought a first-class ticket for *Titanic* and took with him a bag filled with vials of his latest perfumes, which he hoped to market in the US. He left these behind when the boat started sinking and he was rescued on Lifeboat 3. Amazingly, the vials were discovered in 2000 on the seabed, perfectly preserved. They were later used to create a range of modern perfumes based on those original scents.

Danger Ahead

As evening approached, conditions on the Atlantic became more and more icy. At this point some minor precautions were taken.

The captain ordered the ship to head 26 km south before turning towards New York. But he did not reduce its speed. However, lookouts up in the crow's nest were asked to keep an eye out for large icebergs. It was a clear night and the crew believed there would be lots of time to spot any possible dangers and to get out of the way if necessary.

INTO THE ICE

After four days of steady progress, the ship, as warned, entered an ice field. Yet no one on board was particularly alarmed. In fact, many people at the time thought that ice posed no danger to big ships. Before the trip, *Titanic's* captain had been quoted as saying: "I cannot imagine any condition which would cause a ship to founder. Modern shipbuilding has gone beyond that." Indeed, a ship called the SS *Kronprinz Wilhelm* had hit an iceberg head on in 1907. Despite severe damage to its **bow**, it had not sunk.

Most of an iceberg lies beneath the surface.

LOOKOUTS

There were six lookouts on *Titanic*, who took it in turns manning the crow's nest. On 14 April, at 11.40 p.m., Frederick Fleet, the lookout on duty, spotted what he thought was a small iceberg straight ahead. As the ship got closer, however, he realized it was much bigger than he first thought, so he rang the warning bell. This was the first sign anyone on board knew something was wrong.

The ship's warning bell was found in the 1980s.

Titanic's bridge

THE OFFICERS

The captain was so confident that all was well that he had retired to his cabin just after 9 p.m. Another officer had gone to the officers' quarters. This meant that at the vital moment, as the ship headed straight for the iceberg, just four officers were on the bridge. It has long been debated whether the captain's presence on the bridge would have made any difference to the outcome.

EVASIVE ACTION

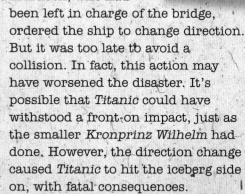

When informed of the iceberg's presence First Officer William Murdoch, who had been left in charge of the bridge, ordered the ship to change direction. But it was too late to avoid a collision. In fact, this action may have worsened the disaster. It's possible that *Titanic* could have withstood a front-on impact, just as the smaller *Kronprinz Wilhelm* had done. However, the direction change caused *Titanic* to hit the iceberg side on, with fatal consequences.

THE BINOCULAR'S STORY

Second Officer David Blair sailed on *Titanic* from Belfast to Southampton and was due to be on its transatlantic crossing. However, a last-minute officer reshuffle led to one of the crew from *Titanic's* sister ship, *Olympic*, taking Blair's place. In the confusion, Blair took with him the key to the cupboard that contained the lookout binoculars. Some believe this contributed to the disaster. Others claim that binoculars would not have been much use in the conditions faced by *Titanic*.

Binoculars recovered from the wreck of *Titanic*

Disaster Strikes

At around 11.40 p.m., *Titanic* struck a large iceberg. At first no one realized how serious the impact was. Most survivors remembered feeling a bump, but nothing more.

However, unknown to anyone on board, the iceberg had done enormous damage to the underside of the ship, and it had begun to sink. Once this realization set in, officers sent up distress rockets while the telegraph operators tried desperately to contact any ships in the area.

THE IMPACT

Unable to get out of the way in time, the ship's starboard side hit the iceberg. Although around 30 m of the iceberg could be seen above the water, towering over the deck, no damage was reported to the ship's upper levels. However, around 90 per cent of an iceberg's mass is underwater – and that was where the damage was caused. The iceberg gouged a series of holes in *Titanic's* hull below the waterline. Five of its 'watertight' compartments began filling with water, and the ship started to sink, bow first.

DISTRESS SIGNALS

Earlier in the evening a nearby ship, the *Californian*, had telegraphed an ice warning to *Titanic*. But by the time *Titanic* started sinking, the *Californian's* crew had gone to bed. On *Titanic*, Fourth Officer Boxhall tried to attract the attention of the ship by sending rocket distress signals soaring 75 m into the air. They were seen by lookouts on the *Californian*, but when woken up and informed, the captain chose to ignore them. He was heavily criticized for his actions after the disaster.

Titanic sent up distress rockets.

CQD TO SOS

Realizing that the ship was in serious danger, the *Titanic* telegraph operator Jack Phillips started urgently sending messages asking for help from any ships that might be in the area. He sent the then most commonly used Morse code distress signal, **CQD**. A new Morse code signal, **SOS**, had been introduced a few years before, but it had not yet been widely adopted. Encouraged by his assistant operator, Phillips became the first person to transmit the SOS signal from a ship.

Telegram from the *Titanic* to *Olympic*

Telegram announcing *Titanic* is sinking

THE ICEBERG'S STORY

The iceberg that destroyed *Titanic* would have begun life around 15,000 years ago as snowfall on a glacier on Greenland's west coast. Gradually the snow would have been packed down till it formed hard glacial ice. Once this part of the glacier reached the sea, an enormous chunk would have broken off, or calved, to form an iceberg. The berg, believed to have been around 1.6 km long, would then have been slowly carried by tides and currents out into the ocean and into the path of the oncoming ship.

Photo believed by some to show the iceberg that sank *Titanic*.

Abandon Ship!

After the impact, Captain Smith and the ship's designer, Thomas Andrews, inspected the damage below decks. Realizing how serious the situation was, the captain ordered the lifeboats to be prepared and for passengers to start evacuating the ship.

Unfortunately, there weren't enough lifeboats for everybody on board. A lack of training (since there hadn't been a lifeboat drill) and a general air of confusion and panic meant that many boats were launched before they were full.

LIFEJACKETS

There should have been a lifejacket for everyone on board. However, many people weren't able to find theirs in the panic. The jackets were designed to keep a fully clothed person afloat, but they gave no protection against the cold. Down in the bowels of the ship, not all of the gates separating third class from the rest of the ship had been opened, leaving many people trapped inside.

THE LIFEBOATS

White Star Line's lifeboat policy was another sign of its overconfidence in *Titanic*. There weren't enough boats for all the passengers – the regulations of the time didn't state that there had to be. There were 16 solid lifeboats (numbered 1–16) and four collapsible lifeboats (lettered A–D) with room for 1,178 people. Unfortunately, there were 2,223 people on board. Furthermore, because a lifeboat drill had been cancelled none of the passengers had a clear idea of what they were supposed to be doing as the disaster unfolded.

WOMEN AND CHILDREN FIRST

The lifeboats began to be lowered at 12.45 a.m., just over an hour after the impact, beginning with Lifeboat 7. It was a chaotic process. According to the ship's rules, women and children were supposed to take their places first. However, quite a few men made their way on to the boats before all the women and children had been taken care of. Panic soon began to take hold, and officers were forced to fire shots in the air to stop people rushing the lifeboat.

KEEPING CALM

Not everyone panicked. Father Thomas Byles, a Catholic priest from Yorkshire, was walking on the top deck when ship struck the iceberg. He helped many third-class passengers get into the lifeboats, but he refused a place for himself. Instead, he stayed on deck, saying prayers and listening to passengers' confessions until the ship went down.

The crew helped passengers flee *Titanic's* decks.

LAUNCHED HALF FULL

Poor training meant that the officers and able seamen in charge of the lifeboats didn't know they could be launched fully loaded. As a result, many were put in the sea with far fewer people than they could actually hold. Lifeboat 1 carried just 12 people, although it had room for 40. This greatly increased the number of fatalities. Despite the evidence all around them, some people still didn't think the ship would sink – or, at least, not before help arrived – and stayed on deck.

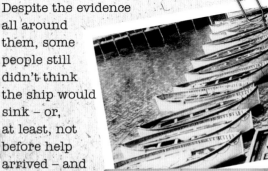

Lifeboats recovered after the disaster.

THE BUSINESSMAN'S STORY

Born into a successful mining family, Benjamin Guggenheim was one of the richest people on *Titanic*. He was travelling with his mistress, her maid and his valet in first class. After the collision, he put on casual clothes and escorted the women on deck where they boarded a lifeboat. Realizing they would be unable to escape too, Guggenheim and his valet returned to their cabins and changed into formal evening dress. They then went and waited in the foyer of the grand staircase to 'go down like gentlemen'.

All Benjamin Guggenheim's wealth couldn't save him.

A Ship Destroyed

*T*itanic, the 'unsinkable' ship, slipped beneath the waves just 2 hours and 40 minutes after its deadly collision with the iceberg. The people on the lifeboats now had to wait for help.

They drifted in the freezing darkness, hoping that someone had received the ship's distress signals and was on their way to rescue them. Those that hadn't made it on to a lifeboat either went down with the ship or jumped into the water. A few were able to swim their way to a lifeboat. But most were quickly overcome by the cold and died in the icy black waters.

THE SHIP GOES UNDER

The ship's bow, which had received most of the damage in the collision, quickly began to fill with water. It started sinking into the ocean, raising the **stern** in the air and tipping screaming, terrified people into the sea. By 2 a.m., *Titanic* was almost vertical. Its lights went out soon after and its funnels broke off. The ship then split in two with a dreadful crash around two thirds of the way down its length. The bow section sank almost immediately. However, the stern section briefly righted itself, before it too dropped beneath the waves.

Sketch of *Titanic* splitting in half and sinking, made by survivor John B. Thayer

A lifeboat searching for survivors

CAST ADRIFT

Passengers in lifeboats began to row away from the disaster area. Only one of the 20 lifeboats, number 14, commanded by Fifth Officer Lowe, went back to pick up people from the sea, rescuing four more. Afterwards, after widespread public anger, some of the survivors claimed they hadn't gone back because they were afraid of being sucked down by the sinking *Titanic*. Others said they feared their boats would be swamped if they took on more people from the water, and everyone would die.

SAVING THEMSELVES

Not everyone who didn't make it into a lifeboat on board *Titanic* died. Some of those who jumped into the water were able to cling on to debris from the ship, such as deckchairs, and make their way to lifeboats. Around 40 in total fought their way to Collapsible Lifeboats A and B, which hadn't launched properly and were lying upside down in the water. Many, however, died of hypothermia before they could reach safety, usually within just 20 minutes of hitting the water.

THE QUARTERMASTER'S STORY

It was First Officer Murdoch who gave the order for the ship to change direction when the iceberg came into view. However, it was Quartermaster Robert Hitchens who actually turned the wheel, for which he gained the nickname 'the man who sank *Titanic*'. Later he took charge of Lifeboat 6, but was widely criticized by his fellow survivors. They accused him of refusing to go back to help people in the water and of bullying those in the boat.

Quartermaster Robert Hitchens

Rescuing the Survivors

The closest ship to *Titanic*, *Californian*, didn't respond to its distress signals. Thankfully the *Carpathia*, which was nearly 100 km away, did.

Having received the messages sent by *Titanic's* telegraph operators, the *Carpathia's* captain ordered his crew to head to the site of the disaster to try to rescue as many passengers as possible. Around four hours later, the *Carpathia* had arrived on the scene. It managed to save 706 people. The other 1,517 passengers of *Titanic* died.

ROWING FOR THEIR LIVES

As fast as the *Carpathia* was travelling, Captain Rostron still had to worry about the icy conditions – he didn't want his ship to suffer the same fate as *Titanic*. In fact, it proved too icy and unsafe for the *Carpathia* to enter the ice field where the *Titanic* had sunk. Instead, the ship held its position and waited while the survivors rowed their lifeboats to it.

Survivors being winched aboard *Carpathia*

THE *CARPATHIA* ARRIVES

The *Carpathia* was a transatlantic passenger ship travelling from the Mediterranean to New York. When it received *Titanic's* distress signal at around 12.25 a.m., it was 93 km from the disaster area. The captain, Arthur Rostron, had the ship turn round and race towards *Titanic*. He also ordered his crew to prepare food, clothes and rooms for any survivors they might find. When the ship arrived at 4 a.m., *Titanic* was already on the seabed.

The captain of *Carpathia*, Arthur Rostron

Back on Board

At 4.10 a.m., the first lifeboat, number 2, reached *Carpathia*. The first survivor to be taken on board was first-class passenger Elizabeth Allen, a US citizen. It took a further four hours for all the lifeboats to reach *Carpathia*. The boat then set sail for New York. As they boarded, the survivors were wrapped in blankets and given hot food and drinks. Many were also reunited with their loved ones, while others discovered the terrible news that their friends and family hadn't made it.

Passengers on *Carpathia* help *Titanic's* survivors

Medal awarded to a *Carpathia* crewmember

Giving Thanks

Titanic's survivors were so grateful for the actions of Captain Rostron and his crew that they pooled their money to buy them a silver cup. Each of the *Carpathia's* 320 crewmembers was also presented with a bronze, silver or gold medal. On the front was a picture of the *Carpathia* sailing through the ice fields. On the back was the following inscription: "Presented to the captain, officers and crew of RMS *Carpathia* in recognition of gallant and heroic service from the survivors of SS *Titanic*."

Molly's Story

The US millionaire Margaret 'Molly' Brown was in Lifeboat 6, commanded by Robert Hitchens. They had several heated arguments. Hitchens thought the boat should remain where it was so it could be found easily, while Brown though the passengers should row to keep warm. Apparently, Hitchens also claimed that the approaching *Carpathia* was not there to rescue them but to "pick up dead bodies." Brown threatened to throw Hitchens overboard and got everyone to row towards the ship. She was later hailed as a hero and given the nickname 'unsinkable Molly Brown'.

Titanic's survivors row towards *Carpathia*.

Arrival in
New York

Three days after the disaster, on 18 April 1912, *Carpathia* delivered the survivors of *Titanic* into New York. There was a crowd of 40,000 people to greet them.

Titanic's distress signals had been picked up in Canada and word of the disaster had soon spread. In fact, it quickly became the biggest story of the year, dominating newspaper headlines around the world for weeks. Inquiries into the events began almost immediately in the US and UK. Both put forward recommendations that have prevented a similar tragedy from happening again.

READ ALL ABOUT IT

In the first few days, there were few hard facts for the newspapers to report. *Carpathia's* captain had maintained radio silence for two days, refusing to answer questions from the press. He didn't confirm what had happened until Wednesday 17th. But a lack of information didn't stop the papers from printing (often very inaccurate) stories. The Monday edition of the *New York Evening Sun* even claimed that all the passengers had been saved and the liner was being towed back to shore.

AGONIZING WAIT

For relatives of those on board, the days after the disaster were agonizing as they waited for news of their loved ones. Crowds gathered at the offices of the White Star Line in London, Southampton and New York. On Wednesday 17 April, the company began publishing lists of survivors, but these were often incomplete and sometimes had names spelled incorrectly. Some families had to wait weeks before discovering the truth.

Newsboy announces the disaster outside White Star Line's London offices

The US inquiry into *Titanic's* sinking

INQUIRIES

The US inquiry into the disaster began just four days after the tragedy. The British inquiry got going a couple of weeks later. Both reached largely the same conclusions and called for a range of safety requirements for future liner travel. However, there were some differences. The Americans placed the blame for the disaster on Captain Smith for his 'overconfidence and neglect', while the Brits didn't find anyone personally responsible.

Operating the radio on a simulator of a modern ship

LESSONS LEARNED

ICE PATROL

In 1914, Canada, the US and countries in western Europe came together to found the International Ice Patrol (IPP), which still operates today. Using boats and planes operated by the US Coastguard, it monitors the presence of ice and icebergs in the Atlantic. It then sends the data to every ship in the area so that they can change their course if necessary. Since the IPP's introduction, no similar tragedy has occurred.

LIFEBOATS

One of the most important – and obvious – recommendations of both inquiries was that all ships should have enough lifeboats for everyone on board. For existing ships, this meant placing boats on the decks, reducing the amount of space for passengers. New ships incorporated the extra lifeboats into their design. The inquiries also insisted that the crew was properly trained in how to use the lifeboats and that regular drills were held with passengers.

RADIO CONTACT

Regarded during the first few days of *Titanic's* trip as a bit of a novelty, the radio telegraph proved its worth once disaster struck. It if hadn't been installed, it's possible that no ship could have been contacted to come to *Titanic's* rescue, resulting in even greater loss of life. The inquiries recommended that all ships should be fitted with communication radios that would operate 24 hours a day.

A patrol ship passes near two icebergs.

Yellow lifeboats lining the side of a giant modern liner

THE BAKER'S STORY

Charles John Joughin was *Titanic's* head baker. When the evacuation of the *Titanic* began, he helped passengers into the lifeboats but didn't board one himself. Instead he went to the rear of the ship and 'rode' it down as it sank, finally stepping into the water just as *Titanic* dropped beneath the waves. He is believed to be the last survivor to leave the ship. He then trod water for around two hours before hauling himself on to the upturned collapsible Lifeboat B, where other survivors were clinging on.

Victims and Survivors

It's generally accepted that there were 1706 survivors of *Titanic*. However, it's not known for certain how many died because the ship's crew and passenger lists are thought to be inaccurate.

The US inquiry put the number at 1,517. What is known for certain is that more third-class passengers died than first-class ones. As the ship went down, the crew went to work saving the first-class and second-class passengers, while those in third class were largely left to look after their own survival.

RECOVERING THE DEAD

Once *Carpathia* had returned to New York with the survivors, other ships were sent to perform the much more unpleasant task of recovering the dead. Launched from Halifax, Canada, they were loaded with ice and coffins and carried professional **embalmers**. In total, 328 bodies were found, of which 119 were buried at sea. The rest were returned to shore where 59 were claimed by families. The others were buried in cemeteries in Halifax.

THE SURVIVORS

It's believed that around 60 per cent of passengers in first class, 42 per cent of passengers of second class, but only 25 per cent of passengers in third class survived. Third-class passengers faced the largest obstacles in trying to escape. Their accommodation was furthest from the lifeboats, the gates separating third class from the rest of the ship had not all been opened, and the crew gave greater priority to first- and second-class passengers for spaces on the lifeboats.

Class	Survived	Died
First	199	130
Second	119	166
Third	174	536
Crew	214	685

BRAVE BECKER

Ruth Becker was just 12 years old when she boarded *Titanic*. Travelling with her mother, brother and sister, she became separated from them in the confusion of the evacuation. They were placed in Lifeboat 12, while she was on Lifeboat 13. There she showed great bravery, helping to calm the other passengers and handing out blankets. She was reunited with her family on *Carpathia*. She didn't get on a boat again until 1990, at the age of 90, when she took a cruise to Mexico.

THE YOUNGEST SURVIVOR

Millvina Dean was just seven weeks old at the time of the tragedy, making her the youngest survivor. Her mother and brother also survived, but her father, who had wanted to be a tobacconist in the US, died. The mother decided not to stay in the States and sailed the family back across the Atlantic to England just a month after the tragedy. Millvina lived to be 97, becoming the last passenger of *Titanic* to die in 2009.

Honeymooners Mr and Mrs Harder aboard *Carpathia*.

NEWLY-WEDS

For several newly married couples, a trip aboard *Titanic* formed part of their honeymoon. Tragically, the 'women and children first' rule meant that many new brides never saw their husbands again. However, some couples did make it. First-class passengers George and Dorothy Harder escaped together in Lifeboat 5, while second-class couple Ethel and Edward Beane did the same in Lifeboat 13 – eventually. Edward was initially refused permission to board. However, seeing that the boat was not full, he jumped into the water once it had launched and swam to safety.

THE COUPLE'S STORY

Isidor Strauss, the extremely wealthy German-born owner of Macy's department store in New York, travelled on *Titanic* with his wife Ida. When the ship began to sink, Ida refused to get into a lifeboat without her husband, saying: "We have lived together for many years. Where you go, I go." They were last seen standing together on the ship's deck.

Mackay-Bennett, one of the ships used to recover bodies from the ocean

Letter authorizing Isidor Strauss's nephew to take charge of the body recovered by *Mackay-Bennett*.

Discovering
Titanic

For 73 years, the wreck of *Titanic* lay undiscovered and undisturbed at the bottom of the ocean.

Various attempts were made to find it without success. Part of the problem was that *Titanic's* final location had not been accurately recorded in 1912, so everyone was looking in the wrong place. It was also so far down that for many decades the technology to reach it simply didn't exist. Finally, in 1985, a team led by the US **underwater archaeologist** Robert Ballard found the ship using an unmanned **submersible** called *Argo*.

THE LOST SHIP

Even before the wreck had been found, people were coming up with ideas of what to do with it. Some proposed turning it into a memorial for those who lost their lives in the tragedy. Others wanted to bring it back to the surface. In 1914, an American architect called Charles Saville put forward a plan for raising *Titanic* using magnets. In the late 1970s, a film exploring a similar idea, *Raise the Titanic* was made. It wasn't very successful and lost a lot of money. As its producer famously said, "It would have been cheaper to lower the Atlantic."

The film *Raise the Titanic* imagined the ship being brought back to the surface.

Once they said
God himself couldn't sink her.
Then they said
no man on earth could reach her.
Now—you will be there when we...

RAISE THE TITANIC

THE SEARCH FOR THE SHIP

Until the 1980s, no expedition had come close to finding *Titanic*. Robert Ballard succeeded in 1985, not just because he knew that the original location had been reported incorrectly, but because he was able to use a US Navy remote-controlled submersible to search the sea floor. Even so, for two months, Ballard and his team didn't find anything. Then, on 1 September, the ship finally came into view. It was lying around 770 km south-east of Canada at a depth of about 3,800 m.

The submersible *Argo* searches the ocean floor.

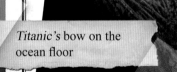
Titanic's bow on the ocean floor

FOUND AT LAST

The ship was lying on the seabed overlooking a small canyon – since named Titanic Canyon. The bow and stern sections were still upright but lay far apart from each other, confirming that the ship had split in half on the surface. The bow was much better preserved than the stern, which was a crumpled mess of steel and wood. Around the wreck is a forest of debris made up of broken pieces of the ship and passengers' belongings covering an area 8 by 5 km.

One of the first photos of the wreck, taken in 1985

PRECIOUS ARTEFACTS

A manned French submersible, *Nautile*, visited the wreck in 1987. It used robotic arms to gather hundreds of artefacts, including porthole windows, leather bags and statues. Since then, many more expeditions have taken place and thousands of items have been brought to the surface. These range from passengers' possessions, such as jewellery, clothes, boots, and children's marbles to parts of the ship, including crockery, doors, lifeboat davits (lowering mechanisms), the ship's compass and even a 17-tonne section of the hull.

A selection of artefacts rescued from the wreck of *Titanic*

THE BACTERIA'S STORY

The destruction of *Titanic* isn't quite over yet. Scientists have discovered that it's being eaten away by iron-feeding bacteria. These bacteria have created rusticles – long icicle-like structures made of rust – all over the ship's body. The damage is so great that some experts believe that the remaining structure of *Titanic* will collapse into dust in around 50 years or so.

The Most Famous Ship in the World

Over 100 years since the event, the sinking of *Titanic* continues to have a powerful hold on the public imagination.

The story has taken on a new life in popular culture, retold in many different ways – in films, TV shows, musicals and video games. Thousands of books have been written to catalogue every detail of the tragedy, and to tell the tales of almost everyone involved. The name 'Titanic' itself has become a byword for a disaster caused by human arrogance.

REMEMBERING THE SHIP

From the first silent films to the latest 3D video games that allow players to virtually explore the ship, *Titanic's* appeal to the public has never weakened. Within a few days of its sinking, newspapers and magazines were producing special *Titanic* editions, packed with photos and first-hand stories. In-depth books, films and TV shows followed, examining the story from every angle. The entertainment industry has kept the story of the ship alive for each new generation to rediscover.

Nearer, My God, to Thee.

There let my way appear,
Steps unto heaven,
All that Thou sendest me
In mercy given.
Angels to beckon me,
Nearer, my God, to Thee,
Nearer to Thee.

THE SILENT FILM

Perhaps the most astonishing of all the many films made about *Titanic* was the very first one. It starred Dorothy Gibson, an American silent-movie actress who was travelling back from a holiday in Europe on – and was rescued from – *Titanic*. Gibson co-wrote and starred in *Saved from the Titanic* just a month after her ordeal. In the film she wore the exact same clothes she'd worn on board the ship.

The film star, and *Titanic* survivor, Dorothy Gibson

Sheet music of songs associated with the *Titanic*

A NIGHT TO REMEMBER

One of the most popular books about *Titanic* was Walter Lord's *A Night to Remember*, published in 1955. As a boy, Lord had taken a trip on Titanic's sister ship, *Olympic*, which had inspired his later interest in the tragedy. In order to make his account as accurate as possible, Lord interviewed dozens of survivors. In 1958, the book was turned into a successful film.

Kenneth MORE in
A NIGHT TO REMEMBER

A still from the film showing passengers scrambling into the lifeboats

THE POWER OF SONG

There have been two stage musicals written about *Titanic*. The first in 1960, *The Unsinkable Molly Brown*, focused on the heroic actions of one of the survivors, Margaret Brown (see p. 37). The second, which opened in New York in 1997, was called simply *Titanic*. Its story touched on the different experiences of first- and third-class passengers, and included songs entitled 'The Largest Floating Object in the World' and 'To the Lifeboats'.

PLAYBILL
a weekly magazine for theatregoers
Winter Garden
THE UNSINKABLE MOLLY BROWN

THE DIRECTOR'S STORY

In the 1997 film *Titanic*, directed by James Cameron, a giant model ship and a 17-million-gallon water tank were used to recreate the disaster. A number of problems during filming meant the production went over schedule and was vastly over budget. It ended up costing $200 million, making it the most expensive film made at that time. Many critics thought it was bound to be a failure. However, when it opened, it immediately became a smash hit. Drawing record audiences, it became the highest-grossing film of all time, taking more than $2 billion worldwide. It has since been surpassed *Avatar*, which was also directed by James Cameron.

LEONARDO DiCAPRIO   KATE WINSLET

NOTHING ON EARTH COULD COME BETWEEN THEM

TITANIC
FROM THE DIRECTOR OF 'ALIENS', 'T2' AND 'TRUE LIES'

Glossary

Able-bodied seaman
A member of a ship's crew who has been trained to perform certain tasks, such as how to operate a lifeboat.

Bow
The front part of a ship. The rear part of a ship is known as the stern.

Bugler
Someone who plays a bugle, a type of old-fashioned trumpet.

Cargo
Commercial goods that are being transported on a vehicle, such as a lorry, a train, a plane or a ship.

CQD
A distress call used in the early days of the telegraph. CQ was the code for a general call to all telegraph operators, while 'D' stood for 'Distress'. Some people believe it stands for 'Come Quickly, Danger', but this was a later invention.

Crew
The group of people who manage, operate and serve on a ship.

Deck
The horizontal levels on a ship. The top deck acts as the ship's roof. On *Titanic*, this was where the lifeboats were located.

Dormitory
A large bedroom where many people can sleep, usually in single beds or in bunk beds.

Dry dock
A part of a dockyard into which a ship can be sailed. The water can then be drained out to give workers access to the ship's hull.

Embalmer
Someone who uses chemicals to preserve human bodies to stop them from rotting, allowing them to be buried.

Gantry
A large bridge-like structure that supports other pieces of equipment, such as cranes.

Hold
The lower part of a ship's interior where goods and cargo are stored.

Hull
The watertight body of the ship that sits below the surface.

Immigration
Coming to a new country in order to live there.

Inquiry
An official investigation into an incident.

Keel
A long, strong section at the bottom of a ship that supports the frame and hull.

Knot
A unit of speed used by ships. One knot equals 1.85 km/h.

Lifeboat
A boat stored on a bigger boat that can be used by passengers and crew to escape in an emergency.

Liner
A large, luxurious ship that can carry many passengers and travel long distances. These ships used to travel regular routes, or 'lines', which is how they got their name.

Maiden voyage
The first official voyage of a ship.

Morse code
A way of communicating using combinations of short and long sounds (dots and dashes) to represent letters.

Navigate
To work out the route of a vehicle, such as a ship, usually by using maps and various pieces of technology.

Premonition
A strong feeling that something bad is going to happen.

Promenade deck
Titanic had several decks with roofs and open windows where passengers could walk and take the air without getting wet. To promenade means to walk.

Quartermaster
The member of a ship's crew whose main job is to look after the supplies.

Sea trial
A test voyage conducted soon after a ship has been built to see if there are any problems with it.

Slipway
A ramp in a shipyard, situated next to the water where ships are built and launched from.

SOS
The Morse code distress signal that replaced CQD. Although many people believe the letters stand for 'Save Our Souls', they don't actually stand for anything. They were chosen simply because they were easy to send and interpret – three dots, followed by three dashes, followed by three dots.

Starboard
The right-hand side of a ship (when facing toward the bow). The left-hand side is known as port.

Stern
The rear part of a ship. The front part is known as the bow.

Stoker
A member of the ship's crew whose job is to feed (or stoke) a boiler with coal.

Submersible
A craft designed to operate deep underwater. Submersibles can be either manned or unmanned.

Telegraph
A way of transmitting messages using electrical signals, usually in Morse code. Early telegraphs were made up of networks of wires. *Titanic's* telegraph was wireless. It transmitted messages using radio waves.

Turkish bath
A type of sauna or steam bath that is popular in Turkey.

Underwater archaeologist
Someone who studies historic remains and artefacts discovered on the sea floor.

This is a Carlton book

Copyright © Carlton Books Limited 2015

Published in 2015 by Carlton Books Ltd
An imprint of the Carlton
Publishing Group
20 Mortimer Street, London W1T 3JW

10 9 8 7 6 5 4 3 2 1

A catalogue record for this book is available from the British Library.

ISBN 978 1 78312 149 6

Printed in China

Senior Editor: Alexandra Koken
Senior Art Editor: Rebecca Wildman
Design: Andy Jones
Picture Research: Emma Copestake
Production: Charlotte Cade

Index

PICTURE CREDITS

The publishers would like to thank the following sources for their kind permission to reproduce the pictures in this book.

Key: t=Top, b=Bottom, c=Centre, l=Left and r=Right.
Page 1 Carlton Books; 2-3 Popperfoto/Getty Image; 3r Time Life Pictures/Getty Images; 4t Shutterstock; 4b Roger Viollet/Getty Images; 4-5c Universal Images Group/Getty Images; 5tl Wikimedia Commons; 5tr Hulton Archive/Getty Images; 5b Wikimedia Commons; 6-7(background) Wikimedia Commons; 6-7t Emmanuel Dunand/Getty Images; 6b Wikimedia Commons; 7tr Hulton Archive/Getty Images; 7c WENN Ltd/Alamy; 7bl Popperfoto/Getty Images; 8-9 De Agostini Picture Library/getty Images; 9l Universal Images Group/Getty Images; 9r Wikimedia Commons; 10t Albert Harlingue/Getty Images; 10b Kevin Walsh Nostalgia Collection/Mary Evans Picture Library; 11tl Paul Popper/Popperfoto/Getty Images; 11tr Wikimedia Commons; 11bl Wikimedia Commons; 11br John Moore/Getty Images; 12t Universal Images Group/Getty Images; 12b Photo Researchers/Mary Evans Picture Library; 13t Topical Press Agency/Getty Images; 13c Onslow Auctions Limited/Mary Evans Picture Library; 13b The Illustrated London News Ltd/Mary Evans Picture Library; 13r Time Life Pictures/Getty Images; 14t Universal Images Group/Getty Images; 14b Dorling Kindersley/Getty Images; 15t Bettmann/Corbis; 15l Popperfoto/Getty Images; 15r Mary Evans Picture Library/Alamy; 16 Popperfoto/Getty Images; 17t Wikimedia Commons; 17b Dorling Kindersley/Getty Images; 18-19(background) Carlton Books; 18r Splash/Henry-aldridge.co.uk/Splash News/Corbis; 19tl Onslow Auctions Limited/Mary Evans Picture Library; 19tr Wikimedia Commons; 19c Epa European pressphoto agency b.v./Alamy; 20-21 Carlton Books; 21tl Archive Pics/Alamy; 21tr Illustrated London News Ltd/Mary Evans Picture Library; 21cr Illustrated London News Ltd/Mary Evans Picture Library; 21bl Universal Images Group/Getty Images; 22(background) Onslow Auctions Limited/Mary Evans Picture Library; 22tr Onslow Auctions Limited/Mary Evans Picture Library; 23l Barcroft/Getty Images; 23tr Peter Dazeley/Getty Images; 23c Topham Picturepoint/Topfoto; 23br Colville/Hulton Archive/Getty Images; 24t Wikimedia Commons; 24c Topham Picturepoint/Topfoto; 24b Wikimedia Commons; 25tl Matt Cardy/Getty Images; 25tc Wikimedia Commons; 25bl Wikimedia Commons; 25cr Brian Harris/Alamy; 25br Brian Harris/Alamy; 26l Onslow Auctions Limited/Mary Evans Picture Library; 26r Wikimedia Commons; 27tl Wikimedia Commons; 27tr Mike Marsland/Getty Images; 27bl Wikimedia Commons; 27br Tony Kyriacou/Rex Features; 28r Shutterstock; 29tl Archive Pics/Alamy; 29tc Topham Picturepoint/Topfoto; 29tr Illustrated London News Ltd/Mary Evans Picture Library; 29bl David Sandison/The Independent/Rex Features; 29br Don Emmert/Getty Images; 30 Hulton Archive/Getty Images; 31tr Dpa-Film 20th century fox/DPA/Press Association Images; 31tl Matt Campbell/AFP/Getty Images; 31bl Popperfoto/Getty Images; 31br Barcroft/Getty Images; 32tr Leon Neal/AFP/Getty Images; 32br Hulton Archive/Getty Images; 33l Wikimedia Commons; 33c Time & Life Pictures/Getty Images; 33r Print Collector/Hulton Archive/Getty Images; 33br Ullstein bild/Getty Images; 34l SSPL/Getty Images; 34-35 Dorling Kindersley/Getty Images; 35tl Universal Images Group/Getty Images; 35tr Universal Images Group/Getty Images; 35br Wikimedia Commons; 36-37(background) Hulton Archive/Getty Images; 36l Universal Images Group/Getty Images; 36tr Universal Images Group/Getty Images; 37tl Universal Images Group/Getty Images; 37c Richard Gardner/Rex Features; 37br World History Archive/Alamy; 38tr FPG/Getty Images; 38br Print Collector/Hulton Archive/Getty Images; 39tl Stock Montage/Getty Images; 39tr Imagno/Getty Images; 39cr Bruno Vincent/Getty Images; 39br Wikimedia Commons; 39bl Monty Rakusen/Getty Images; 40 The Granger Collection/Topfoto; 41tl Wikimedia Commons; 41tr Gerry Penny/AFP/Getty Images; 41cl Mary Evans Picture Library/Alamy; 41c Wikimedia Commons; 41br Phil Yeomans/Rex Features; 42 (background) Emory Kristof/Getty Images; 42r ITV/Rex Features; 43tl Ralph White/Corbis; 43tr SSPL/Getty Images; 43cr AFP/Getty Images; 43br Emory Kristof/Getty Images; 43l Sipa Press/Rex Features; 43c Joel Saget/AFP/Getty Images; 44 (background) Shutterstock; 44l Wikimedia Commons; 44c Culture Club/Hulton Archive/Getty Images; 44tl Everett Collection Historical/Alamy; 44bl Mary Evans Picture Library/Alamy; 45tl Universal History Archive/Getty Images; 45tr John Pratt/Getty Images; 45cl Mander and Mitchenson/ArenaPAL/Topfoto; 45bl Archive Photos/Moviepix/Getty Images; 45cr AF Archive/Alamy; 45br Hector Mata/AFP/Getty Images.

Every effort has been made to acknowledge correctly and contact the source and/or copyright holder of each picture and Carlton Books Limited apologises for any unintentional errors or omissions, which will be corrected in future editions of this book.